Original title:
Holding On to Love

Copyright © 2024 Swan Charm
All rights reserved.

Author: Paulina Pähkel
ISBN HARDBACK: 978-9916-89-610-5
ISBN PAPERBACK: 978-9916-89-611-2
ISBN EBOOK: 978-9916-89-612-9

Emblazoned in Memory

Whispers of laughter echo bright,
In corners where shadows dance at night.
Every moment stitched with care,
A tapestry of love laid bare.

Fleeting glances, soft and warm,
Hold the essence, a calming charm.
Time once lost, now a symbol true,
Emblazoned in memory, me and you.

In the Garden of Us

Where petals bloom in fiery hues,
We wander beneath the vast blue.
Hands intertwined, hearts aligned,
In this garden, love defined.

Sunlight dances on tender leaves,
In every rustle, a promise weaves.
A fragrant breeze carries our song,
In the garden of us, we belong.

Along the Winding Path

Footsteps trace the winding way,
With every turn, new sights display.
Side by side, we share the view,
The journey's sweet, just me and you.

Through the thicket and gentle stream,
We find the magic, share the dream.
With every step, our spirits soar,
Along the winding path, explore.

The Glow of Shared Dreams

In twilight's hush, our hopes ignite,
Casting shadows in the fading light.
With whispered wishes, we awake,
The glow of dreams, the love we make.

Stars align in the velvet sky,
With every heartbeat, we can fly.
Together, we chase the starlit gleam,
In the glow of our shared dream.

A Bouquet of Shared Seasons

In spring we found the blooming flowers,
With colors bright, they danced for hours.
Summer brought the sun's warm glow,
Filling our hearts with joy to grow.

Autumn's leaves, a golden blaze,
Whispered tales of fleeting days.
Winter wrapped us in soft white,
Creating peace in silent night.

The Nest We Built Together

We gathered twigs and woven dreams,
Constructed walls with gentle beams.
A cozy place where love resides,
With open hearts and arms as guides.

Through storms we held, through winds we stood,
Our nest a shelter, strong and good.
In every corner, laughter rang,
Together we found the joy to hang.

Secrets Carried on the Breeze

Soft whispers float on twilight air,
Stories shared without a care.
The breeze, a messenger of trust,
Carrying dreams, a sacred must.

Underneath the stars so bright,
We exchanged our hopes each night.
With every gust, our spirits soared,
Finding solace, our hearts adored.

Shadows Dancing in Soft Light

In the glow of evening's crest,
Shadows twirl, a moving fest.
Figures merge, then take their flight,
In a dance of soft moonlight.

Each flicker tells a tale untold,
Of memories cherished, bright and bold.
As darkness deepens, dreams ignite,
Shadows whisper in the night.

Emblems of Our Affection

In whispers soft, our secrets dwell,
Tales of love only time can tell.
With every touch, a story spins,
Emblems of warmth, where comfort begins.

Under starlit skies, our dreams align,
A gentle rhythm, your heart in mine.
Through laughter shared and sorrows borne,
Together we rise, through dusk and dawn.

In simple gestures, our truths unfold,
A silent promise, more precious than gold.
In every glance, a universe stirs,
Emblems of love, in whispered blurs.

As seasons change, our roots run deep,
In quiet moments, awake from sleep.
Hand in hand, through thick and thin,
Emblems of love, forever akin.

So raise a toast to the bonds we weave,
In every heartbeat, we choose to believe.
With eyes that gleam, and spirits bright,
Emblems of our affection, shining light.

Crumbs of Joy Along the Way

In morning sun, we chase our dreams,
With optimism, our laughter beams.
Each step we take, a path unwinds,
Crumbs of joy left behind.

In shared moments, we find our place,
Warmed by love, kindness, and grace.
A smile exchanged, small treasures found,
Crumbs of joy, in hearts abound.

As shadows dance, we walk with cheer,
Through tangled paths, our vision clear.
With every hug, hope's gentle sway,
Crumbs of joy light the way.

In fleeting glances, our spirits intertwine,
A secret thrill, a heart's design.
With every laugh, we softly say,
Crumbs of joy along the way.

So gather close, and share your light,
In simple gestures, hearts take flight.
With every moment, let love convey,
Crumbs of joy, here to stay.

Unfading Echoes

In shadows deep, the memories sing,
Whispers of laughter, a delicate ring.
Time holds them close, like stars in the night,
They dance in the silence, a soft, glowing light.

Where echoes linger, hope finds its way,
A tapestry woven, come what may.
Footsteps retraced on a well-trodden path,
The heart beats softly, avoiding the wrath.

In corners forgotten, joy still resides,
Like petals of roses, where beauty abides.
Fading yet vibrant, each note is a skein,
Unfurling the stories that whisper again.

Beneath the moon's gaze, in the twilight's embrace,
Dreams interwoven, a fragile lace.
Through time's gentle passage, they endlessly flow,
In the echoes of love, forever we'll grow.

When Hearts Take Flight

In moments hushed, where dreams unfold,
Hearts whisper secrets, both tender and bold.
Like birds in the dawn, they rise on the breeze,
Soaring together, with effortless ease.

With every heartbeat, a story is spun,
Two souls entwined, where adventure begun.
Through valleys of shadows, and mountains of light,
They journey together, igniting the night.

A canvas of stars, painted anew,
Each glance a promise, each touch a clue.
Underneath twilight, their hopes intertwine,
In the beauty of silence, their spirits align.

When hearts take flight, the world fades away,
Every barrier crumbles, there's nothing to sway.
With laughter and tears, they learn how to dance,
Two souls in the sky, lost in romance.

As seasons may change, love stays the same,
Boundless and fearless, it cannot be tame.
With wings made of dreams, they embrace the unknown,
In the vastness of love, they've both found a home.

A Serenade for Two

In the hush of the night, a melody glows,
Two hearts in harmony, the soft music flows.
With every note played, a story is spun,
A serenade whispers, we're never alone.

Under the stars, where shadows entwine,
The world fades away, just your hand in mine.
With laughter and sighs, our souls start to soar,
In this dance of the night, we are bound evermore.

Each breath a connection, a bond we uphold,
The warmth of our presence, a comfort so bold.
Through verses and rhymes, we find our sweet place,
In the music of love, we'll endlessly trace.

In quiet moments, our hearts softly sway,
A serenade lingers, come what may.
With dreams intertwined, our spirits take flight,
In every soft whisper, we'll conquer the night.

As dawn casts its glow, and the night fades away,
The song of our hearts will forever replay.
Together we'll dance, in life's tender hue,
With the rhythm of love, a serenade for two.

The Flame That Guides

In the darkest of nights, when shadows are cast,
A flame flickers softly, a beacon steadfast.
With whispers of courage, it warms the soul,
Leading the weary, making them whole.

Through storms that may come, it dances with grace,
Lighting the path, in this endless chase.
With each gentle flicker, it sings to the heart,
Reminding the lost that they're not far apart.

In moments of doubt, when the road feels long,
The flame that guides us, becomes our song.
Its glow shines bright, like a promise so true,
With love as the fuel, we'll always break through.

As embers rest quietly, dreams start to rise,
Building a future beneath endless skies.
In the heart of the night, when all seems to fade,
The flame that guides us, in unison swayed.

And when dawn arrives, with its golden light,
The flame's gentle warmth will still hold us tight.
In the journey ahead, through the trials we'll stride,
With love as our compass, the flame that guides.

An Odyssey of Hearts

In every glance, a story shared,
Two souls entwined, a journey dared.
Through trials faced, and laughter found,
Together we dance on sacred ground.

The stars align, a cosmic guide,
With whispered dreams, we will not hide.
With every heartbeat, we explore,
The endless path, forevermore.

Through valleys deep and mountains tall,
We rise as one, we will not fall.
In tender moments, trust will bloom,
Love lights the way, dispels the gloom.

Hand in hand, we dare to roam,
In every heart, we find our home.
An odyssey so rich and bold,
A tale of love, forever told.

Nature's Embrace of Us

Beneath the sky, where whispers play,
Nature cradles us each day.
The rustling leaves, a gentle sigh,
In harmony, we learn to fly.

Sunlight dances on our skin,
With every breath, the world spins thin.
Mountains rise, oceans greet,
In nature's arms, our hearts compete.

The winding rivers, soft and clear,
Guide us closer, year by year.
With petals bright, and fragrances sweet,
In nature's song, we feel complete.

Storms may come, and shadows fall,
Yet hand in hand, we conquer all.
In every cycle, love renews,
Nature's embrace forever clues.

The Alchemy of Us

From simple sparks, a fire ignites,
In the alchemy of shared delights.
With whispered secrets, our spirits blend,
Two hearts become more than just friends.

Through trials faced, and dreams we weave,
In the golden threads, we shall believe.
With every touch, the magic grows,
In the dance of love, our spirit glows.

The moonlight casts a silver hue,
In every moment, a bond so true.
Transforming pain into sweet relief,
In alchemy, we shed our grief.

Together we stand, come what may,
In this enchanted, timeless play.
In laughter and in tears, we trust,
For in our hearts, there's only us.

Waves of Comfort on the Shore

The ocean whispers, soft and clear,
Calling us close, drawing us near.
With gentle waves, the tides embrace,
In every splash, we find our place.

Footprints linger in the sand,
As nature writes with tender hand.
The sun sets low, a fiery glow,
In waves of comfort, feelings flow.

Seagulls dance in the evening air,
With every breath, we shed our care.
The rhythm beats like a heart's own song,
In this sacred space, we belong.

Hand in hand, we greet the night,
With stars above, the world feels right.
The ocean's lull, a soothing shore,
In waves of comfort, forevermore.

Cradled in Timelessness

In the hush of twilight's glow,
Moments linger, soft and slow.
Whispers dance on gentle air,
Life's embrace beyond compare.

Past and future intertwined,
In this space, peace we find.
Echoes of the heart reside,
Cradled here, time is a guide.

Stars above with stories bold,
Tales of warmth, a love untold.
Together, we shall remain,
In this timeless, sweet refrain.

Glimmers of a day once bright,
Held forever in the night.
Cradled in the arms of fate,
Timeless love, we celebrate.

So let the worlds fade away,
In this moment, come what may.
Cradled in a gentle dream,
Life flows softly, like a stream.

The Glimmer of Tomorrow's Dreams

In a world that paints the skies,
Hope ignites with each sunrise.
With hearts open wide and free,
We reach for what we cannot see.

Tomorrow glimmers in our eyes,
Woven threads of sweet goodbyes.
Every dream a star that gleams,
Guiding us through whispered themes.

With every step, we chase the light,
Turning shadows into bright.
For in the dawn, we find our voice,
In the future, we rejoice.

Together, hand in hand we walk,
Sharing every silent talk.
The dreams of tomorrow call our name,
In our hearts, they spark a flame.

So let us dance, beneath the moon,
With each heartbeat, we find tune.
The glimmer shines, a beacon bold,
Tomorrow's dreams, forever told.

Fables Woven with Hope

Once upon a time, they say,
In a land where shadows play.
Fables told by firelight,
Woven tales that spark the night.

Each story carries dreams anew,
Of knights and realms where hearts are true.
With courage strong and hope as guide,
In every truth, our fears abide.

Through the pages, laughter swells,
In the lines, where magic dwells.
Woven threads of joy and pain,
Stories linger, love's refrain.

With each fable, lessons learned,
In the heart, a fire burned.
Hope, a beacon shining bright,
Guides our souls from wrong to right.

So gather round, and share your tale,
Let hope's breeze fill every sail.
Fables woven with love and light,
Guide us through the darkest night.

Cascading Rays of Belief

In the dawn, the light cascades,
Softly through the golden glades.
Each ray a whisper, a new day,
Guiding paths along the way.

With every step, belief unfolds,
In the heart, a courage bold.
Follow dreams, let shadows flee,
Embrace the warmth of what can be.

Together, we shall rise up high,
Like soaring birds that kiss the sky.
In the myriad of colors bright,
We find our strength, our guiding light.

Each moment, steeped in pure grace,
Paints a smile upon our face.
Cascading rays, a gentle touch,
Remind us we are loved so much.

So when the world feels vast and cold,
Let the light of hope be bold.
Cascading rays ignite the dawn,
In our hearts, the dreams live on.

Embracing the Light of Us

In the dawn's soft embrace,
We find warmth in our glow.
Together we rise and chase,
A path only we know.

With each whisper of the breeze,
Our dreams dance in the air.
Two souls pledged to believe,
In a love forever rare.

Through shadows we will tread,
Hand in hand, side by side.
In the light, we are led,
With hope as our guide.

With colors bright and bold,
We paint a world anew.
In stories yet untold,
Our hearts will carry through.

Together we ignite,
The flame of love's pure trust.
In this beautiful light,
We are, and always must.

Echoes of Our Heartbeats

In the quiet of the night,
Your heartbeats blend with mine.
A rhythm, soft and light,
In perfect, sweet design.

Through the alleys of our dreams,
We wander hand in hand.
Each echo softly seems,
To speak love's magic brand.

With every laugh and sigh,
We resonate as one.
Under the starlit sky,
Together we have spun.

In moments, lost in time,
Our pulses softly blend.
A gentle, soothing rhyme,
Where heart and soul transcend.

In the depths of this love,
We find solace and peace.
Forever, just above,
Our heartbeats never cease.

The Canvas of Us Intertwined

With brushes dipped in dreams,
We create our own fate.
Colors burst at the seams,
A love that can't wait.

In splashes of the night,
Our passions come alive.
Each stroke a pure delight,
In art, we both thrive.

With every line we draw,
Together we define.
We break each daunting flaw,
In harmony, we shine.

We dance in hues so bright,
As shadows fade away.
This canvas feels so right,
In each and every sway.

As all our visions meet,
In union soft and grand,
This masterpiece, so sweet,
Reflects our hearts, our hands.

Starlit Dreams of Togetherness

Beneath the silver skies,
We weave our dreams tonight.
With every glance, we rise,
In starlight, pure and bright.

Together, hand in hand,
We wander through the night.
In this enchanted land,
Our spirits take to flight.

With whispers soft and clear,
Each star holds our embrace.
In silence, we draw near,
To find our sacred space.

With wishes set afloat,
In constellations wide,
Our hearts sing every note,
In this vast space, we glide.

As twilight fades to dawn,
We keep the dreams alive.
In love's soft light, we're drawn,
Together we will thrive.

Whispers of the Heart

In the quiet of night,
Soft sighs drift on air,
Secrets dance in shadows,
Dreams whisper a prayer.

With every heartbeat's thrum,
Love's echo finds its way,
Through the veils of longing,
Where hopes dare to stay.

Eyes meet amidst silence,
A language so divine,
Unspoken yet vivid,
In hearts, we intertwine.

With the stars as our guide,
We wander through this space,
Each moment a treasure,
In time's warm embrace.

The heart speaks in whispers,
A tune sweetly played,
In the stillness of night,
Our fears gently fade.

The Tapestry of Us

Threads of laughter woven,
In colors bright and bold,
Each memory a stitch,
In stories yet untold.

Through the highs and the lows,
Together we will stand,
With every twist and turn,
We weave hand in hand.

Moments blend like shades,
In a canvas of dreams,
United in our journey,
Nothing's as it seems.

The fabric of our lives,
Rich with love and grace,
In every shared heartbeat,
We find our true place.

In the tapestry of us,
Each detail finely spun,
A masterpiece of souls,
Forever we are one.

In the Embrace of Tomorrow

Fingers trace the dawn,
As light begins to play,
In the embrace of hope,
We welcome a new day.

Promises kissed by sun,
A future bright and clear,
With every breath we take,
Joy eclipses all fear.

Through the shadows we rise,
With dreams set ablaze,
In unity we march,
Towards bright, endless days.

The horizon calls softly,
With whispers of our fate,
In the warmth of tomorrow,
We find love's true weight.

Together we will stand,
As the world spins around,
In the embrace of tomorrow,
Our hearts will be found.

Clinging to Moments

In the dance of seconds,
Time slips through our hands,
We gather up the fragments,
Like grains of golden sands.

Each laugh, a fleeting spark,
Each tear, a precious gem,
We cling to these moments,
Like whispers in a hymn.

With the sun setting low,
We cherish the day's light,
In the beauty of stillness,
We hold on through the night.

Memories like petals,
Softly drift in the breeze,
In the garden of our hearts,
They bloom with gentle ease.

Let us treasure each blink,
For they are ours to keep,
In the tapestry of time,
Our love runs deep.

Beneath the Boughs of Belonging

In quiet glades where whispers sway,
Soft sunlight dances, brightening day.
Roots entwined in earth's embrace,
We gather strength, we find our place.

The leaves above, a tapestry,
Threads of life in harmony.
Gentle breezes hum a tune,
Underneath the watching moon.

With every branch, a story told,
Of dreams we share, of hearts so bold.
Beneath the boughs, we laugh and sing,
In this shelter, love takes wing.

The shadows fall, the night descends,
Stars appear as daylight ends.
In this space, we feel so free,
A bond of souls, you and me.

Together here, we pause, we breathe,
In nature's arms, our hearts believe.
With every moment, love reveals,
The strength of roots that time conceals.

Voices of the Heart

In echo chambers, secrets dwell,
Whispers soft, like distant bell.
Rhythms pulse in time with grace,
Voices rise, a warm embrace.

Words unspoken, yet so clear,
Conveying hopes, dispelling fear.
Silent songs, they linger long,
Threading life into our song.

Harmony in every breath,
Celebrating love, defying death.
Vibrations dance around our souls,
Mending hearts, making us whole.

Through tangled paths, we find our way,
Guided by what our hearts say.
In every note, a story starts,
These are the voices of our hearts.

Together through the stormy night,
Turning shadows into light.
In each connection, truth imparts,
The symphony that love imparts.

Celestial Bonds Unbroken

In constellations, stories lie,
Galaxies dance across the sky.
Stars align in perfect time,
Echoing love in silent rhyme.

Comets trail through endless space,
Marking journeys, every trace.
In celestial arms, we soar,
Bound together, forevermore.

Through the dark, we find our way,
Guided by the light of day.
Each twinkle speaks of promise bright,
In the vastness, we ignite.

With every heartbeat, a new star born,
In the silence, our dreams adorned.
Galactic whispers, soft and clear,
In every moment, you are near.

United by our cosmic fate,
In endless orbits, we create.
The universe, an endless sea,
Celestial bonds that set us free.

Serene Shadows of Desire

In twilight's glow, our secrets blend,
Amidst the whispers, we transcend.
Shadows linger, soft and sweet,
In this stillness, lovers meet.

The moonlit path invites our feet,
In darkened corners, passions greet.
Every glance a flame ignites,
In serene shadows, love alights.

Between the lines of silent gazes,
Desires weave through midnight mazes.
With every breath, our souls conspire,
A dance of hearts, a gentle fire.

In the hush of night, we find our way,
Guided by stars that softly sway.
With secrets shared, our spirits rise,
In serene shadows, love never dies.

Together we explore the night,
Wrapped in dreams, a pure delight.
In every heartbeat, desires bloom,
Amid the shadows, love's sweet room.

Ties That Bind

In shadows cast, our hands entwined,
Whispers shared, a silent kind.
Through storms we weather, side by side,
With every heartbeat, love won't hide.

Moments stitched with threads so fine,
In each embrace, our souls align.
Through time and space, we find our way,
Two hearts as one, come what may.

In laughter's echo, joy resounds,
Together, here, our purpose found.
A tapestry of dreams we weave,
In trust and hope, we dare believe.

Beneath the stars, our secrets flow,
A bond unbroken, ever glow.
In silence shared, the truth we'll find,
In every moment, ties that bind.

The Language of Touch

Fingers trace the lines of fate,
In warm caress, we resonate.
A gentle brush, the world unseen,
In silent words, we weave between.

A lingering gaze, a soft embrace,
In every touch, a sacred place.
No need for words, our hearts converse,
In tender glances, love's universe.

Through stormy nights and sunlit days,
Our bodies dance in timeless ways.
In moments shared, we lose control,
The language of touch, it speaks our soul.

A loving hand upon my cheek,
In every sigh, the silence speaks.
In every heartbeat, every shush,
Our love, the language of the hush.

Timeless in Your Eyes

I lose myself in depths so wide,
In every glance, the world aside.
The universe within your gaze,
A timeless dance, a fiery blaze.

In sparkling light, the galaxies spin,
Your eyes, a story, where dreams begin.
Each twinkle holds a hidden gem,
In stillness wrapped, the love we stem.

In every moment, ageless grace,
A canvas bright, your heart's embrace.
With you, I see the past and more,
A future bright, forever shore.

In tender nights, we find our rest,
In dreams entwined, our souls are blessed.
Through endless time, we'll always fly,
Together bound, in each other's eye.

Lanterns in the Dark

When shadows creep, and night draws near,
Your light ignites, dispelling fear.
With every flicker, hope ignites,
Lanterns shining through darkest nights.

Together we chase the fading light,
With hands held tight, in endless flight.
Through winding paths, our spirits soar,
In every heartbeat, we explore.

Each lantern glows, a promise shared,
In every struggle, we're prepared.
With every spark, a wish takes flight,
In love's embrace, we conquer night.

Through storms we dance, through trials tough,
In every moment, we are enough.
With you beside me, all fears depart,
Forever, love, you are my heart.

A Canvas of Heartbeats

In twilight hues, our laughter glows,
Brush strokes of joy, where the river flows.
Each moment etched, a vibrant start,
We paint our dreams from the depths of heart.

Colors blend as we drift and sway,
In this gallery of night and day.
Every heartbeat a note in tune,
A masterpiece kissed by the silver moon.

With each whisper, the canvas grows,
Textures of love in gentle throes.
We dance under stars, a visual art,
Our souls entwined, never to part.

Seasons change, yet still we frame,
Every heartbeat, a drop of flame.
Filled with passions, the colors bright,
A living portrait, pure delight.

So let us create, you and I,
A tapestry woven, reaching the sky.
In every pulse, our story gleams,
A canvas of heartbeats, shared dreams.

A Nest of Memories

In the attic, whispers softly call,
Fragments of laughter, a gentle thrall.
Photographs faded, stories untold,
A nest of memories, woven bold.

Shells from summer, postcards from spring,
Tales of adventures and everything.
Worn out letters, a scent of thyme,
Each little piece, a moment in time.

Wrapped in a quilt, warmth fills the air,
Dreams of tomorrow, beyond compare.
Threading the past with ribbons of grace,
In this cozy nest, we find our place.

Old records playing sweet songs of cheer,
Echoes of love that we hold so dear.
In every crack, a tale we embrace,
A nest of memories, time can't erase.

So here we gather, hearts intertwined,
Treasuring snippets of life we find.
In the soft glow of a fading light,
Our nest of memories shines ever bright.

Fireside Tales of Us

By the fire's glow, stories unfold,
Warmth in our hearts, as the night grows old.
Whispers of dreams wrapped in a cloak,
The flames dance like laughter, piercing the smoke.

Tales of our journeys, both near and far,
Under the gaze of a guiding star.
Every word spun with a golden thread,
Adventures awaken, as we sit and spread.

With cups of cocoa and shadows that play,
We dive into moments that never fray.
Between the crackles, our spirits ignite,
Fireside tales keep the darkness at bay.

Laughter erupts like the sparks that fly,
In the warmth of the stories, we learn to fly.
Together we weave, with each shared glance,
In this circle of trust, there's a sweet romance.

So here's to the nights by the fire's light,
Where our hearts open wide, taking flight.
Fireside tales, forever they will last,
Carved in our souls, a bond unsurpassed.

The Sweetness of Everyday

A quiet morning wrapped in grace,
Sunlight spills on a familiar face.
Coffee brews with a fragrant sigh,
The sweetness of everyday whispers by.

Sidewalks echo with casual chats,
Children's laughter, the sound of hats.
Each simple moment, a treasure to find,
The sweetness of everyday, all intertwined.

Colors of flowers bloom in a row,
Gentle reminders of love that grows.
Every glance shared, a soft ballet,
A rhythm of bliss in the light of day.

Hands intertwined as we stroll along,
Listening close to our heart's sweet song.
Joy lives in details, in subtle ways,
The sweetness of everyday forever stays.

So let us savor this life we weave,
Amidst the mundane, we opt to believe.
For in each heartbeat, simplicity's play,
Lies the everlasting sweetness of everyday.

A Haven Crafted from Dreams

In twilight's embrace, dreams take flight,
Whispers of hope in the soft moonlight.
Each star a wish, glimmers above,
A sanctuary built with threads of love.

Through valleys deep and mountains high,
Our hearts intertwine, we learn to fly.
With every step, a new path unfolds,
Crafting a haven that beauty holds.

Laughter echoes in the gentle breeze,
Memories linger among the trees.
Together we dance on this canvas wide,
A refuge where our spirits reside.

Through storms that rage and shadows that loom,
In this haven, we banish the gloom.
With courage as our guiding light,
We forge ahead, ready to fight.

For dreams are the roots of our unyielding hopes,
A tapestry woven, the fabric of hopes.
In this sacred space, our souls are embraced,
A haven of dreams, forever we chase.

Petals Underfoot

Upon the ground, petals swirl and dance,
Each color a memory, a fleeting glance.
Nature's confetti, soft under our feet,
Every step taken is a moment sweet.

In gardens of laughter, where silence sings,
Time seems to pause as the joy it brings.
With hands intertwined, we wander and roam,
Finding in petals, a place called home.

As seasons shift, what once was now fades,
Yet in our hearts, the beauty cascades.
For even in loss, new buds shall bloom,
A cycle unbroken, no room for gloom.

Through the golden hues of autumn's glow,
We tread softly, where memories flow.
The essence of love, in each petal found,
Reminding us gently, we share common ground.

So let us rejoice with every new dawn,
The petals beneath us, forever live on.
For love's the fragrance, sweet and complete,
In this journey together, life's bittersweet.

Heartbeats in Harmony

In the quiet moments when time stands still,
Two hearts play a symphony, a gentle thrill.
With every heartbeat, a rhythm divine,
Together we dance, our souls intertwine.

Through laughter and tears, through joy and strife,
We compose our song, the melody of life.
In the ebb and flow, we find our way,
Each note a promise, forever to stay.

With hands clasped tight in the gentle night,
Our heartbeats echo, a guiding light.
In the tender moments, where love flows free,
We are the music, the harmony.

Though storms may come and skies turn gray,
Our love's sweet song will never sway.
For in each heartbeat, we breathe as one,
In this waltz of life, we've joyfully spun.

So let our hearts beat as drums of affection,
Together, forever, a deep connection.
In perfect unison, through thick and thin,
With love as our guide, we always win.

The Glow of Unwavering Faith

In shadows deep where doubts may creep,
A flicker remains, a promise to keep.
With every breath, the light breaks through,
A beacon of hope, steadfast and true.

Through trials faced, unwavering we stand,
With faith as our compass, hand in hand.
The journey may wane, but trust stays aglow,
In the darkest of nights, our spirits will grow.

For every stumble, there's grace to be found,
Within our hearts, love's echoing sound.
We rise from ashes, renewed and strong,
In the glow of our faith, we always belong.

So let the winds howl and the storms rage,
In this journey of life, we'll turn the page.
With each step forward, together we tread,
Guided by faith, where the light has led.

With open hearts, we embrace what's ahead,
In the glow of our faith, no words left unsaid.
For in every challenge, love's light remains,
A testament bright, through joys and pains.

The Art of Remembering

In the quiet of the night, we hold,
Fragments of tales that once were told.
Faces and laughter linger in air,
A tapestry woven with utmost care.

Memories like stars, they softly gleam,
Flickers of joy, we chase and dream.
Each heartbeat whispers, a gentle reign,
In the garden of thoughts, love remains.

Captured moments, an artist's brush,
Softly painted strokes in a timeless hush.
Colors of sorrow and joy entwined,
Echoes of past in the heart defined.

Time may fade the edges of sight,
But the core of us burns ever bright.
In the canvas of life, we find our way,
The art of remembering is here to stay.

In shadows of dusk, the past will sing,
A melody sweet, a comforting ring.
Holding us close in soft embrace,
Each recollection, a sacred place.

Shadows of Sweetness

In the golden glow of the setting sun,
Whispers of laughter, two hearts as one.
Moments shared in nature's delight,
Shadows of sweetness dance in the light.

Petals of dreams, soft on the breeze,
Brushes of love that set the heart free.
In twilight's arms, we find our grace,
Soft echoes linger, a warm embrace.

Candied hopes wrapped in tender sighs,
Counting the stardust that fills our skies.
Sweetness flows in the simplest of things,
In every heartbeat, the joy it brings.

Through fields of memories, hand held tight,
Navigating darkness, we chase the light.
In shadows of sweetness, forever we'll roam,
Creating a world that feels like home.

With every sunset, a promise made,
In the dance of the dusk, love won't fade.
In gentle vibrations of softest tune,
We savor the sweetness, morning to noon.

Anchored in Each Other

In turbulent tides, we find our way,
Anchored in love, come what may.
Storms may test the strength of our bond,
But together we rise, creating a pond.

With every challenge, our roots grow deep,
In the garden of trust, we joyfully leap.
Seas may rise and the winds may blow,
Yet anchored in each other, we continue to grow.

With every heartbeat, we cherish the past,
Moments like anchors that steadfastly last.
Navigating futures with hands intertwined,
Through waves and currents, our hearts aligned.

In the calm of twilight, we share a sigh,
Gazing at stars, painted in the sky.
Finding our solace in the soft evening glow,
Together we'll journey, wherever we go.

Anchored in dreams, we softly dare,
To sail through the storms, with love as our air.
In the vastness of life, together we'll stand,
Anchored in each other, a steadfast hand.

Beneath the Weight of Time

Each tick of the clock, a whisper of fate,
Beneath the weight of time, we navigate.
Moments like echoes, they rise and fall,
In the tapestry of life, we hear their call.

Memory's embrace, both gentle and fierce,
Shaping our paths, every joy it pierces.
Bound by the minutes, we dance and sway,
In the shadows of moments, we find our way.

With a glance, a touch, the world slows down,
In the stillness of now, we wear time's crown.
Through laughter and tears, through darkness and light,
We craft a story, holding on tight.

Time may be fleeting, like grains of sand,
Yet in every heartbeat, we understand.
Beneath the weight, we'll find our song,
In the arms of forever, where we belong.

So let us embrace the rhythm we find,
Beneath the weight of time, our hearts aligned.
With every note played in life's grand design,
We'll dance through the ages, eternally entwined.

The Charm of Unseen Connections

In shadows where whispers dwell,
Lies a magic we can't quell.
Threads of fate weave near and far,
Binding souls like a star.

Glimpses shared in fleeting looks,
Stories alight in silent books.
Hearts may drift like leaves in flight,
Yet pulse strong in the night.

With every laugh and sigh we share,
The world feels lighter, filled with care.
Invisible ties that never sever,
Connecting us now and forever.

In crowded rooms, we find our space,
A dance, a spark, a hidden grace.
Unseen lines draw paths anew,
In this charm, I find you.

Together we twine, side by side,
In the currents where we glide.
Through the silence, truth still sings,
The charm of unseen connections brings.

The Language of Silent Gaze

Eyes that shimmer, worlds collide,
A glance that speaks where words divide.
In this quiet, we define,
Emotions pure, a sweet design.

When lips are sealed, the heart will spark,
A silent code lighting the dark.
Every blink, a subtle nod,
Life's symphony, a silent prod.

In crowded hallways, we communicate,
A universe in every fate.
Through tender looks, we understand,
The language traced by heart and hand.

Like sunlit beams on autumn leaves,
In stillness, our spirit weaves.
Within the gaze, a promise bright,
A world unveiled in soft twilight.

With every stare, a story grows,
In silence, deeper pulsing flows.
In the space our eyes create,
The language of love, it resonates.

Heartstrings intertwined

Like vines that twist and twine below,
Our hearts connect with an undertow.
In melody, we find our song,
In this bond, forever strong.

Each beat a rhythm, soft and true,
Echoes that draw me close to you.
In laughter shared, our spirits soar,
Heartstrings intertwined, forevermore.

Through trials faced and joys we share,
In every glance, a silent prayer.
Unified in dreams we chase,
Together we carve our sacred space.

In moments small, in grand designs,
We trace our path in tangled lines.
Through stormy seas or sunny skies,
Our heartstrings sing; love never dies.

A tapestry of life we weave,
In every heartbeat, we believe.
In whispers soft, our faith aligns,
In love's embrace, heartstrings intertwine.

Journeys upon the Wind

Across the skies, our dreams take flight,
Carried by winds, from day to night.
On whispered breezes, we unfold,
A tale of journeys yet untold.

With every gust, a chance to roam,
Adventures call, we find our home.
On paths unseen, where spirits soar,
The wind invites us to explore.

Through valleys deep and mountains high,
In every breath, we touch the sky.
Where whispers dance on nature's breath,
In this journey, life finds depth.

Uncharted routes and footprints left,
Stories carved in nature's heft.
Boundless horizons hold our dreams,
In the wild, we hear the themes.

So let us wander, wild and free,
On journeys marked by destiny.
With hearts alight and spirits bright,
We chase the wind, our guiding light.

Anchors of the Soul

In the stillness of the night,
We find our steady ground,
The whispers of the heart,
In silence, we are found.

Roots that hold us firm and tight,
Against the winds that blow,
Through storms that may cause fright,
Our inner light will glow.

Moments shared and memories made,
Threads of love entwine,
In the fabric of our days,
Connection we define.

When shadows stretch and linger long,
We lift each other high,
Together in this sacred place,
We learn to touch the sky.

With faith as our guiding star,
We sail on seas unknown,
Anchored by the warmth of love,
In unity, we've grown.

Radiance Beneath the Storm

Clouds may gather, skies may gray,
Yet hope still finds a way,
For in the darkest hour,
Our spirits learn to sway.

Raindrops dance upon the ground,
They whisper soft and low,
The heart beats strong and true,
With every ebb and flow.

Through thunder's mighty roar,
We stand with heads held high,
A light within ignites,
No reason to deny.

In the tempest's furious grip,
We find our inner fire,
A spark that guides us through,
We rise and never tire.

For when the storm has passed us by,
A rainbow will ascend,
A promise of tomorrow,
A world anew to mend.

Seasons of Our Heart

Spring whispers secrets of new life,
Awakening our dreams,
With blossoms rich and bright,
Hope flows like gentle streams.

Summer's warmth envelops all,
With laughter in the air,
Long days stretch out like memories,
A tapestry to share.

Autumn leaves begin to fall,
Reminders of the past,
With every hue and shade,
Our hearts beat strong and fast.

Winter's chill may bring us close,
In cozy, quiet nights,
The hearth of love ignites the soul,
With warmth that feels so right.

In each season's tender turn,
We find our story's grace,
A journey through the changing tides,
In every time and place.

The Tapestry of Togetherness

In threads of gold and silver spun,
We weave our lives as one,
With laughter stitched in joy,
And sorrows left undone.

Each moment shared, a pattern bright,
With colors bold and true,
In the fabric of our days,
Our hearts become the hue.

Though frayed and worn at times we fade,
We stand and mend the seams,
With love's embrace, we find our place,
And cherish all our dreams.

Through trials faced and joys embraced,
The beauty lies within,
In every thread that binds us close,
Together, we begin.

A tapestry of souls entwined,
A legacy of light,
Through every stitch of history,
We dance into the night.

The Fire That Ignites Our Souls

In the night, a flame does glow,
Whispers of passion, embers flow.
Hearts ablaze, together we dance,
In this warmth, we find our chance.

Through trials fierce, our spirits rise,
With every spark, love never dies.
Fanning the flames, our souls unite,
Guided gently by the light.

A firestorm brews in the heart's core,
Igniting dreams we've yet to explore.
In its glow, fears fade away,
Together we'll find a brighter day.

Feel the heat that fuels our bliss,
A tender touch, an ardent kiss.
In this warmth, we craft our fate,
The fire within, we celebrate.

With every heartbeat, the flame does grow,
A beacon of love, forever aglow.
In the ashes, we'll find our role,
Together, the fire ignites our soul.

From Ashes to Flourishing Gardens

From the embers, life starts anew,
Buds emerge, kissed by dew.
Ashes scattered, the past set free,
In sunlight's warmth, we find the key.

Roots entwined in the fertile ground,
In silent strength, our hearts resound.
With every seed, a promise blooms,
In vibrant colors, hope resumes.

Once charred remains, now lush and bright,
Turning darkness into light.
Through seasons' change, we learn to grow,
In every challenge, love will show.

Petals flourish, fragrance in the air,
In this garden, we shall share.
From ashes, beauty takes its stand,
Together, we'll nurture this land.

And when the storms of life do test,
In gentle rain, we find our rest.
From ashes, trust, and love collide,
In flourishing gardens, we abide.

Bridges Built on Dreams

Between our hearts, a bridge does span,
With beams of hope, we made a plan.
Each step we take, together as one,
In sunlight's glow, we chase our fun.

With every dream, a plank is laid,
In shared ambition, fears will fade.
We rise above, hand in hand,
Our vision clear, a future planned.

The path may twist, the winds may roar,
Yet on this bridge, we explore.
With courage strong, our dreams take flight,
Guided by stars in the night.

As shadows fall, we will endure,
With every heartbeat, love is pure.
Together we'll make each dream a quest,
With bridges built, we find our rest.

So here we stand, a journey starts,
In the landscape of our hearts.
With every step, we pave the way,
On bridges built, we'll always stay.

The Auras of Our Affection

In silken light, our spirits merge,
A dance of colors, love's sweet surge.
With every glance, a warm embrace,
The auras shine, in time and space.

In laughter's glow, the world feels bright,
Together we chase the softest light.
Fingers entwined, a gentle weave,
In this moment, we dare to believe.

Shadows may fall, yet we remain,
In hues of trust, we break each chain.
Through trials faced, our bonds grow strong,
In the chorus of love, we belong.

The colors shift, yet never fade,
In this spectrum, our dreams are laid.
Across the skies, our spirits fly,
In the auras of love, we'll never die.

As twilight falls, the stars appear,
In this connection, all is clear.
With hearts ablaze, we chase our fate,
In the auras of affection, we create.

Sweetly Grounded

In gardens where the flowers bloom,
The earth's embrace dispels all gloom.
Roots entwined in love's soft thread,
A whispered peace where dreams are fed.

Beneath the sky, the sun will smile,
Inviting souls to linger awhile.
The fragrant winds that dance and play,
Sweetly remind us of this day.

Through seasons' change, the bond remains,
In gentle touch, no need for chains.
For nature teaches hearts to share,
The joy of living, pure and rare.

With every petal, every leaf,
Life finds its rhythm, joy and grief.
Together, rooted, we will stand,
Sweetly grounded, hand in hand.

The Ties That Weather

Through storms that shake and winds that howl,
We find our strength, we lift our vow.
In every trial that life may choose,
The ties we share, we'll never lose.

Like branches swaying in the breeze,
We bend and sway with graceful ease.
In every challenge, heart to heart,
The love we share won't drift apart.

Time may test with shadows long,
Yet through it all, we're still so strong.
With every raindrop, every tear,
Our bond grows tighter, year by year.

A tapestry of trust is sewn,
In every moment, love is grown.
Together facing all the weather,
We'll find our way, now and forever.

A Map of Warmth

In corners bright where kindness glows,
A map of warmth where laughter flows.
Beneath the stars, our hearts take flight,
Illuminating the darkest night.

We trace our paths through valleys low,
With every step, together we grow.
Moments shared, like sunlight's dance,
Create a bond, a sweet romance.

The compass held within our embrace,
Guides us true, keeps up the pace.
In gentle whispers, dreams come alive,
A map of warmth, where spirits thrive.

Through winding roads, both rough and smooth,
With every heartbeat, we find our groove.
Hand in hand, we'll forge our way,
A journey bright, come what may.

Imperishable Glances

In fleeting moments, eyes will meet,
A spark ignites; our souls repeat.
Within a glance, the world can shift,
Imperishable, a timeless gift.

Through crowded rooms, a silent call,
With just one look, we rise or fall.
The magic wrapped in every stare,
Holds stories deep, a secret lair.

In tender silences, hearts align,
Each imperishable glance divine.
A language spoken without a word,
A whispered truth, so often heard.

Amidst the noise, we find our peace,
As fleeting moments seem to cease.
In eyes that shine and smiles that dance,
We find forever in a glance.

Caress of Time's Embrace

Whispers of dawn greet the day,
A soft touch that fades away.
Moments linger, then they flee,
Time's embrace, a mystery.

Shadows dance in golden light,
Memories hold us, burning bright.
Fleeting joys, they come and go,
In the stillness, we learn to grow.

Seasons change, yet hearts remain,
Through the laughter and the pain.
Softly held by time's sweet grace,
In every tear, a warm embrace.

Time's caress, a gentle guide,
In its arms, we live and abide.
Each heartbeat sings a silent rhyme,
Bound forever, in time's climb.

With every tick, a story told,
In moments fleeting, life unfolds.
In time's embrace, together we find,
The threads of love that bind our minds.

Symphony of Shared Moments

In the quiet, we find our song,
A melody that feels so strong.
With every glance, a note we play,
In harmony, we drift away.

Shared laughter echoes in the air,
Moments woven, beyond compare.
A gentle touch, a knowing smile,
Together, we walk each mile.

Through the storms and sunny skies,
Our symphony never dies.
Each memory, a vibrant chord,
In this life, we can't be ignored.

Time may pass, but we will stay,
In this dance, we find our way.
Every heartbeat, a striking rhyme,
In our love, there is no time.

So let us sing, hand in hand,
A symphony that will withstand.
With every note, we sing anew,
In this song, it's me and you.

Twilight's Embrace of Us

In twilight's glow, we softly stand,
With shadows wrapped around our hands.
Whispers float on the evening breeze,
In this moment, hearts find ease.

Stars awaken in deepening skies,
Reflections dance in your loving eyes.
The world fades to a gentle hum,
In twilight's embrace, we become.

Crickets serenade the fading light,
Holding tight, we stay tonight.
Each breath is filled with dreams untold,
In this embrace, we break the mold.

The night drapes softly, a velvet shawl,
In quiet whispers, we hear the call.
Together under the celestial dome,
In twilight's embrace, we feel at home.

As day gives way to the night's sweet song,
In love's embrace, we both belong.
With every heartbeat, we fade away,
In the twilight, forever we stay.

Threads of Joy and Sorrow

Weave through the fabric of our days,
Threads of joy in varied ways.
Each smile brightens the hidden pain,
In life's tapestry, we remain.

Moments stitched with tears and laughter,
Echoes of dreams that chase thereafter.
Through the weft of hopes and fears,
We find strength across the years.

In shadows cast by fleeting light,
We embrace both day and night.
Every thread with stories spun,
Together, we are never done.

Binding joy with sorrow's hue,
Creating a life that's tried and true.
In every stitch, a tale unfolds,
A beautiful journey that we hold.

So let us weave, hand in hand,
Through the mountains and the sand.
For in this life, our hearts entwine,
In threads of love, our souls align.

Infinite Returns

In shadows cast by time's embrace,
The echoes of our laughter trace.
Moments lost, yet always near,
Whispers of a past we hold dear.

Through cycles spun in endless dance,
Life offers us a second chance.
Each heartbeat syncs with dreams we chase,
An infinite loop in timeless space.

Like waves that kiss the shore at night,
Our spirits soar, a shared flight.
In every end, a new begin,
The journey mapped within our skin.

With every turn, we learn and grow,
In love's warm light, we ebb and flow.
Together bound, we find our way,
In infinite returns, we stay.

Embrace the past, the now, the yet,
In moments shared, we won't forget.
For life is but a grand design,
In every heart, a story's sign.

Treasure Beneath the Surface.

Beneath the waves, where silence dwells,
Lies a secret that nature tells.
Glistening gold and pearls so rare,
Waiting for hearts that truly care.

The ocean's depths hold tales untold,
A treasure chest of warmth and cold.
Each grain of sand, a whispering dream,
In the gentle tides, they softly gleam.

Dive beneath the swirling tide,
Where mysteries and wonders hide.
With every stroke, a new delight,
A world awake in soft moonlight.

In the depths, we face our fears,
Through the dark, we find our tears.
But in the treasure, we reclaim,
The hidden parts of love's sweet name.

So take the plunge, explore the seas,
For within the depths lies true degrees.
In every heart, a fate unheard,
A treasure found, a promise stirred.

Gentle Threads of Affection

In quiet moments, hearts entwine,
A tapestry of love, divine.
Each thread a whisper, soft and true,
In gentle light, I see us two.

With every laugh, a color swirls,
In tender hands, the fabric twirls.
Embroidered dreams, a shared delight,
In threads of warmth, we find our light.

The simple acts, a stitch of care,
In every touch, we softly share.
With every glance, a silent song,
In gentle threads, we both belong.

Through storms that rage and winds that howl,
Our woven love, a sacred vow.
With patience, love, we will create,
A masterpiece, our shared fate.

So let us weave this tale so bright,
In vibrant hues of day and night.
For in our hearts, the threads align,
A bond so sweet, forever vine.

Whispered Promises in the Wind

Beneath the moon, where shadows play,
Promises ride on winds that sway.
In every breath, a vow that's shared,
In tender glances, love declared.

The rustling leaves, a soft embrace,
Whispering secrets through time and space.
Each fluttering sound, a hope reborn,
In whispered dreams, a love adorn.

With every gust, our spirits soar,
Captured in winds, forevermore.
Like petals dancing in the breeze,
Our hearts unite, our fears appease.

The nightingale sings of loves unseen,
In twilight skies, we dance serene.
Together bound by threads so fine,
In whispered promises, we align.

So let the winds carry our song,
In unity, we both belong.
For every whisper on the air,
Is love's sweet truth, a timeless care.

The Legacy of Our Laughter

In the air, our joy does soar,
Echoes of giggles, forever more.
Moments wrapped in carefree bliss,
Each one a memory, none we'll miss.

Together under the sun's warm glow,
We shared secrets only we know.
Time danced on, but we stood still,
In laughter's arms, we found our will.

With every chuckle, our bonds grew tight,
Chasing shadows, welcoming light.
We painted colors in shades of glee,
The legacy of us, wild and free.

Though seasons change and ages pass,
Our laughter's echo will always last.
In quiet moments, hear it play,
A melody of love, guiding our way.

So whenever you feel lost at sea,
Remember the joy that once set us free.
For in our hearts, it will remain,
The laughter we shared, our sweetest gain.

Petals on the Breeze of Forever

Softly drift the petals down,
Carried gently, without a frown.
Each a story, each a dream,
Whispers of hope in a sunbeam.

They dance and swirl upon the air,
Fragments of love, rare and fair.
A symphony of colors bright,
Guiding souls through the night.

As time flows like a river wide,
On nature's wings, we'll glide.
From gardens lush to fields unseen,
The journey we take, rich and serene.

Hold onto dreams; let them unfurl,
In the breeze, a hidden pearl.
For life's fleeting and ever dear,
Petals on the breeze, we must steer.

Through the seasons, our hearts will sway,
On the winds of love, we'll play.
The essence of life, in each small part,
Petals and whispers, a work of art.

Silent Whispers Under the Moon

Beneath the glow of the silver light,
Silent whispers of the night take flight.
Stars twinkle softly, secrets shared,
In the stillness, no heart is spared.

The moon hangs low, a watchful eye,
As shadows whisper, time slips by.
In this calm, our dreams unfold,
Stories wrapped in whispers told.

We sit in silence, minds adrift,
The chill of night, a gentle gift.
From depths of dark, we find our peace,
In every sigh, our worries cease.

The air is thick with unsaid words,
A symphony of the night's sweet birds.
Each moment lingers, tender, bright,
In silent whispers, we feel the light.

So let the moon guide our hearts' design,
In silent echoes, our souls entwine.
Forever in this soft embrace,
We find our home, our sacred space.

A Journey Beyond the Horizon

With every step, we chase the dawn,
A journey ahead, a road not drawn.
The horizon calls, whispers our name,
A promise of change, a flicker of flame.

Mountains rise and valleys dip,
The path is winding, a great road trip.
Through forests deep and rivers wide,
We face the unknown, side by side.

Each sunrise paints a brand new sky,
With hopes as vast as the oceans high.
Together we wander, heartbeats in tune,
In the embrace of the brightening moon.

The journey is long, but hearts stay true,
With dreams to light the way, anew.
Beyond the horizon, both strong and free,
In the tapestry of life, just you and me.

With every step into the unknown,
A resounding truth, we've always grown.
For in every moment, in laughter and tears,
We forge our path through the passing years.

A Promise in Polaroid

Captured moments pause the time,
Fleeting smiles, a frame divine.
Whispers of love in each pixel,
Forever held in fragile specul.

In sepia tones, our laughter glows,
Every snapshot a tale that flows.
Memories wrapped in gentle hues,
A promise made, a love to choose.

As seasons change, the pictures fade,
Yet in our hearts, the truths we've laid.
Moments preserved in each embrace,
Life's fleeting joys we can't replace.

With hands entwined, we stand so tall,
These cherished frames, they hold it all.
Through laughter and tears, joy and pain,
In each Polaroid, we'll remain.

So here's to us, in light and shade,
A dance of love that won't evade.
In every click, the world will see,
The promise kept, just you and me.

Vestiges of Togetherness

In quiet corners, shadows play,
Echoes of laughter fill the day.
Handwritten notes in time-worn books,
Remind us here of loving looks.

Stains of coffee, a fragrant trace,
Cups that held our dreams in place.
Seasons passed, yet here we stand,
With vestiges of a life planned.

Footprints linger on the shore,
Waves that crash, yet leave us more.
Each grain of sand, a memory kept,
In tides of time, our secrets crept.

A quilt of moments, stitched with care,
Woven stories, threads we share.
Beneath the stars, our whispers blend,
In every heartbeat, love won't end.

These remnants of our cherished past,
Hold a beauty meant to last.
Through sunsets, dawns, we'll always know,
Together's where our roots will grow.

Wings of Endurance

Beneath the sky, with hearts so wide,
We chase the wind, our dreams collide.
With every flight, through storms we soar,
Unfurling wings, we long for more.

In turbulent skies, we find our grace,
Navigating through every dark space.
The strength we hold, a bond so true,
Together we rise, anew in blue.

Through trials faced, our spirits fly,
On wings of hope, we touch the sky.
With courage forged, our fears take flight,
In endless dawns, we find the light.

In every glance, a promise made,
In every challenge, our fears allayed.
We paint the sky with colors bold,
In stories of wings, our dreams unfold.

So let the breeze guide us along,
In harmony, we'll sing our song.
For love's endurance, our souls embrace,
With wings of fire, we'll find our place.

A Dance in the Rain

Raindrops fall like rhythm's call,
Together we laugh, we rise, we fall.
With every splash, a world anew,
In puddles deep, our joy breaks through.

We spin beneath the clouded lace,
In every twirl, we find our space.
The chill caress, a thrilling thrill,
In nature's arms, our hearts stand still.

As thunder rumbles, we find our beat,
With steadfast steps, we're never beat.
For in this storm, we've found our song,
Through winds of change, we'll carry on.

The air is sweet with earth's embrace,
Each droplet brings a warm grace.
Dance on the streets, let worries wane,
In joyous steps, a dance in the rain.

So here we twirl, in clouds of gray,
With laughter brightening the dismay.
In every heartbeat, we claim our reign,
Together forever, a dance in the rain.

In the Arms of Forever

In whispers soft like twilight glow,
We find our bond, a gentle flow.
Time stands still, as hearts align,
In the arms of forever, you are mine.

With every laugh, a spark ignites,
We dance through days, our pure delights.
A promise made, in starlit skies,
In the arms of forever, love never dies.

Your touch, a balm, in troubled night,
Guiding me home, to purest light.
Together we rise, and together we fall,
In the arms of forever, we have it all.

Through storms we face, and nights so cold,
Our tale is rich, in love retold.
A journey shared, so bold, so true,
In the arms of forever, just me and you.

In dusk and dawn, our spirits soar,
Hand in hand, we yearn for more.
In this embrace, we find our peace,
In the arms of forever, love's sweet release.

Rooted in Your Presence

In gardens grand, where shadows play,
I find my heart, so here I stay.
Your laughter dances on the breeze,
Rooted in your presence, life's sweetest ease.

With every glance, the world feels bright,
Your smile, a beacon, my guiding light.
In every moment, I choose to grow,
Rooted in your presence, love's warm glow.

Through changing seasons, our roots entwine,
Together we flourish, our hearts combine.
In silence shared, or in whispers hushed,
Rooted in your presence, I feel so brushed.

Beneath the stars, we carve our dreams,
Life unfolds in radiant beams.
In every breath, a love so true,
Rooted in your presence, I'm home with you.

With every trial, we stand so tall,
In the strength of us, we can't fall.
In laughter, in tears, forever we face,
Rooted in your presence, my sacred place.

Captured Moments in Time

A snapshot here, a memory rare,
In fleeting glimpses, we find our share.
With every smile, a tale unfolds,
Captured moments in time, our love untold.

Through the lens of life, we frame our days,
In colors bright, love's endless praise.
Each heartbeat echoes, a rhythm divine,
Captured moments in time, forever in line.

In laughter shared and tears we shed,
We weave our stories, where dreams are led.
With every glance, a silent chime,
Captured moments in time, so sublime.

In quiet corners, or grand displays,
Every adventure, our hearts ablaze.
Together we cherish, each sacred rhyme,
Captured moments in time, forever we climb.

With every dusk, we find our dreams,
In silken threads, our memory streams.
In every heartbeat, love's sweet crime,
Captured moments in time, our perfect rhyme.

The Warmth of Our Embrace

When winter winds bring chills and night,
Your arms around me feel so right.
In every heartbeat, my soul finds grace,
In the warmth of our embrace, a sacred space.

Through storms and shadows, we find our way,
In whispered secrets, we choose to stay.
Each gentle touch, a love interlace,
In the warmth of our embrace, we find our place.

As daylight fades, and stars ignite,
Two souls entwined, in soft moonlight.
With every sigh, our fears erase,
In the warmth of our embrace, time drifts apace.

Through trails we blaze, hand in hand,
Our journey shared, a bond so grand.
In every moment, love's sweet trace,
In the warmth of our embrace, we find our grace.

With every flutter, a promise grows,
In tender whispers, love overflows.
In forever's dance, hearts interlace,
In the warmth of our embrace, I find my place.

Echoing Lullabies of Us

In twilight's hush, we softly sigh,
Whispers weave through the evening sky.
Stars awaken, twinkling bright,
Guiding our dreams through the gentle night.

Crickets serenade, a sweet refrain,
Holding our hearts in a tender chain.
Moonlight dances on our drawn-out spells,
Echoing tales that only time tells.

In this quiet, where shadows blend,
Every heartbeat feels like a friend.
Sheltered whispers in a world so vast,
Holding tight to the moments that pass.

As dusk enfolds, we close our eyes,
Wrapped in the warmth of a soft sunrise.
Together in dreams, we drift afar,
Echoing lullabies beneath the stars.

In the stillness, we call it fate,
Every breath smells sweet on the plate.
Harmonies drawn from the threads of grace,
The lullabies echo in time and space.

Moments of Serendipity

Beneath the canopy, we chance a meet,
A flicker of fate in the vibrant street.
An accidental glance, a spark ignites,
Leading our hearts to shared delights.

In crowded rooms where laughter flows,
We find connection that brightly glows.
A simple word can shift the tide,
With every moment, worlds collide.

Coffee spills on a rainy day,
Yet somehow it clears the clouds away.
In the randomness, a truth unfolds,
Life's little secrets are yet to be told.

Stumbling into paths unforeseen,
In these fragments, love can glean.
Every chance encounter, a sacred birth,
Moments of serendipity, gifts of worth.

With laughter's echo and a whispered cheer,
In the tapestry of life, we're woven near.
Each random dance, a step so free,
In this beautiful chaos, you and me.

Pathways of Trust

On winding roads where shadows play,
We weave our stories, day by day.
With every step, a promise made,
In pathways of trust, we aren't afraid.

Hands intertwined, as seasons change,
Through trials and storms, we remain.
Every journey, a lesson learned,
In the fires of life, our spirits burned.

Silent vows beneath the stars,
In every heartbeat, our love is ours.
Together we tread on paths unknown,
With strength in unity, we're never alone.

Through overgrown fields and mountain highs,
With every dawn, a new horizon lies.
In laughter and tears, our hearts align,
In the sanctuary of trust, our souls entwine.

So here's to the journey, both rough and sweet,
In the dance of life, we will not retreat.
With every challenge, our bond grows strong,
In pathways of trust, we truly belong.

The Diary of Our Journey

Each page turned, a tale unfolds,
In the diary of moments, a love that holds.
Beneath the ink, our dreams reside,
Chronicled whispers, side by side.

From first glances to laughter's ring,
The magic that simple memories bring.
In passages written with care and grace,
The journey is carved in time and space.

Every chapter a tapestry sewn,
In words cherished, we've truly grown.
Through laughter and trials, our hearts ignite,
Every entry a beacon, our guiding light.

With every sunset and dawn anew,
In the diary's embrace, I cherish you.
Moments captured, under moon's glow,
A journey in ink, where love continues to flow.

As the pages turn, our story expands,
In the diary of our love, our lives in hand.
From beginnings humble, to stars we chase,
Together we write in this sacred space.

Reflections in a Still Pond

In the water, dreams unfold,
Ripples tell stories untold.
Leaves drift gently on the surface,
A mirror of nature's purpose.

Clouds pass by, a soft embrace,
Sunlight dances with grace.
Time stands still in this repose,
Whispers of peace in gentle prose.

Nature's canvas, pure and bright,
Colors blend from day to night.
Each ripple holds a silent sound,
Echoes of life all around.

Birds alight on branches near,
Their songs carried, crystal clear.
Moments captured, fleeting fast,
Beauty lingers, shadows cast.

In the stillness, hearts connect,
Reflections held with deep respect.
A world within a pond so wide,
In this calm, our joys abide.

When Two Become One

Two paths crossed beneath the sky,
Fates entwined, no need to pry.
Hand in hand, hearts beat as one,
A journey shared, a race begun.

Dreams collide like stars at night,
Together, shining, pure delight.
Every laugh, a melody,
A duet sung in harmony.

Through storms and sunshine, side by side,
In each other, we confide.
Building castles in the sand,
With love's embrace, we take a stand.

Moments woven, time stands still,
With open hearts, our spirits thrill.
Two souls merged in sacred trust,
In togetherness, we find our must.

As seasons change and ages grow,
The bond we share continues to flow.
When two hearts beat with the same tone,
In love's embrace, we're never alone.

Sources of Light Amidst Shadows

In the dark, where whispers tread,
Hope ignites, illuminating dread.
Stars emerge from deep night's cloak,
Their gentle warmth, a soothing stroke.

Flickering flames, a guiding force,
In shadows deep, we find our course.
With each spark, courage grows,
Through trials faced, resilience shows.

Moonlight spills on quiet streets,
A dance of light where darkness meets.
Every heart, a lamp held high,
Together we shine, refuse to die.

In laughter shared, in smiles bright,
We find comfort, banishing fright.
Sources of love, vast and bold,
In unity, warm and untold.

From ashes rise, removing chains,
In light, we find where hope remains.
Amidst the shadows, we embrace,
The strength of love, our saving grace.

The Essence of Our Togetherness

In quiet moments, we convene,
Where laughter trails, and hearts are seen.
With every glance, a story flows,
In gentle whispers, love bestows.

Hands entwined, we walk the path,
Through trials faced and endless laughs.
Each breath shared, a promise made,
In this bond, no fears invade.

The essence of joy, a sacred thread,
Woven tight with words unsaid.
In storms we face, the calm we find,
In togetherness, our hearts aligned.

Morning light spills through our days,
Filling moments in countless ways.
In mirth and sorrow, we stand tall,
The strength of love, our greatest call.

Through life's dance, we twirl and sway,
Creating memories that forever stay.
In every heartbeat, the truth we confess,
The essence of us, a timeless caress.

Threads of Affection

In whispered tones, our stories weave,
Through laughter shared, and hearts believe.
Each moment stitched with care and light,
Binding our souls, an endless flight.

With gentle hands, we pull each thread,
Creating dreams where love is fed.
A tapestry of hopes and fears,
Woven together over the years.

In vibrant colors, our lives align,
Threads of affection, pure and divine.
Together we stand, hand in hand,
In this intricate, vast wonderland.

Through storms we face, and skies so clear,
In every tear, we find what's dear.
The fabric of us, sturdy and true,
Threads of affection, me and you.

So when life pulls, and tensions rise,
We'll hold our ground, we are the ties.
A bond unbroken, forever strong,
In threads of affection, we belong.

Beneath the Starlit Promise

Under a sky where stars ignite,
Whispers of dreams take wing tonight.
In silent vows, our spirits soar,
Beneath the starlit promise, we explore.

With every glance, the world fades away,
Guided by constellations, come what may.
Your hand in mine, a gentle guide,
In this celestial dance, love won't hide.

As moonlight spills on quiet ground,
Our hearts beat strong, a sacred sound.
In the vast expanse, we're never alone,
Beneath the starlit promise, we've grown.

The universe hums a soothing tune,
Under the watchful eye of the moon.
In the night's embrace, we'll find our way,
While starlight whispers what words can't say.

Together we chase the dreams we seek,
In every heartbeat, our souls speak.
Beneath the starlit promise, so bright,
Our love shines on, a radiant light.

Echoes of Warmth

In the stillness, a soft embrace,
Echoes of warmth in this sacred space.
With every heartbeat, the fire glows,
A gentle reminder, our love bestows.

Through whispered secrets and tender sighs,
Our laughter lingers like endless skies.
In moments shared, the world feels right,
Echoes of warmth, our guiding light.

In the twilight, shadows play,
Yet love prevails at the end of the day.
With hands entwined, we face the storm,
In echoes of warmth, our hearts are warm.

Every memory, a treasure bright,
A soft reflection in the moonlight.
Through trials faced, our spirits climb,
Echoes of warmth, through space and time.

So let the night come, let the stars gleam,
In this tranquil world, we dare to dream.
For in the language of love, we find,
Echoes of warmth, hearts intertwined.

Entwined Destinies

In the dance of fate, our paths entwined,
In every moment, the stars aligned.
With gentle grace, the universe spun,
Entwined destinies, two become one.

Through storms we travel, hand in hand,
Guided by love, our gentle command.
In laughter's echo, our spirits play,
Entwined destinies, forever stay.

Each choice we make, a thread in the weave,
In dreams we share, we dare to believe.
Through shadows cast, together we shine,
Entwined destinies, your heart with mine.

As seasons change, our love will grow,
In the tapestry of life, we flow.
Through joy and sorrow, humor and grace,
Entwined destinies, our sacred space.

So here we stand, in this sacred trust,
With dreams unfurled, in love we must.
Bound by a fate so strong, so fine,
Entwined destinies, forever thine.

Fragments of Forever

Time whispers softly, a fleeting song,
Moments held tender, where hearts belong.
Memories shimmer like stars in the night,
Each fragment a story, a spark of light.

Echoes of laughter, shadows of tears,
Together we wander, dismissing our fears.
The past lingers gently, a guiding hand,
In fragments of forever, together we stand.

Winds of the future carry us high,
Drifting on dreams, we learn to fly.
Embracing the echoes of all we've become,
In the tapestry woven, our hearts beat as one.

Each heartbeat a promise, each glance a vow,
In time's gentle passage, we discover how.
The beauty of now, like blossoms in spring,
In fragments of forever, together we sing.

Whispers of love, like a soft caress,
In every fragment, there lies no less.
As time unfolds softly, we still find our way,
In fragments of forever, we choose to stay.

The Gentle Pull

A breeze sweeps softly, through trees it plays,
It carries our dreams, brightening our days.
A gentle pull tugs at the heart's tender thread,
Leading us onward, where hopes are fed.

The moon's silver glow, in the stillness of night,
Draws shadows together, bringing warmth, bringing light.

A dance of the stars, in the vast open sky,
The gentle pull whispers, reminding us why.

The river's calm flow, a melody sweet,
Guiding us onward, where love and life meet.
The gentle pull lingers, a promise it spares,
Through currents we navigate, through joys and through cares.

With each sunrise breaking, a new chapter starts,
The gentle pull echoes in all of our hearts.
In harmony's rhythm, we learn to be free,
Bound to each other, it's you and it's me.

Time flows like water, yet never we stray,
The gentle pull leads us, come what may.
In the dance of existence, we find our own song,
The gentle pull keeps us where we belong.

Chasing Sunlight Together

In fields of green, where the wildflowers sway,
We chase the sunlight, dancing all day.
Laughter like music, a sweet serenade,
Taking each moment, where memories are made.

Shadows grow longer, as the sun dips low,
We wander through whispers of dusk's gentle glow.
In the warmth of each glance, a spark starts to rise,
Chasing sunlight together, under painted skies.

Glimmers of hope in the twilight we find,
In the rush of the evening, our souls intertwined.
Each step a reflection, every sigh a cue,
Chasing sunlight together, just me and you.

The stars twinkle softly, a cosmic embrace,
In the quiet of night, we find our own space.
Though shadows may linger, our hearts will remain,
Chasing sunlight together, through joys and through rain.

Tomorrow awaits, with its promise anew,
The horizon beckons, a vibrant hue.
Together we'll wander, wherever it's bright,
Chasing sunlight together, bathed in pure light.

Stitches of the Past

In the fabric of time, threads intertwine,
Stitches of the past, with purpose align.
Each memory whispered, a tale gently sewn,
In colors of laughter, and shades of our own.

Tattered and aged, yet beautifully worn,
Echoes of moments, where love has been born.
The quilt of our journeys, a warmth we can feel,
Stitches of the past, in memories, heal.

Each patch tells a story, each fold holds a sigh,
In the depths of our heart, beneath the vast sky.
We stitch and we mend, as the years drift along,
Embracing the melodies of our lifelong song.

Amidst all the chaos, in the quiet we find,
The stitches of the past, forever entwined.
In the tapestry woven, love binds us all tight,
Stitches of the past glow with timeless light.

As we gather around, the stories we share,
We thread through each moment, with love and with care.

In the fabric of yesterday, today finds its way,
Stitches of the past shape our life's grand ballet.

Printed in the USA
CPSIA information can be obtained
at www.ICGtesting.com
CBHW061044231124
17857CB00048B/593